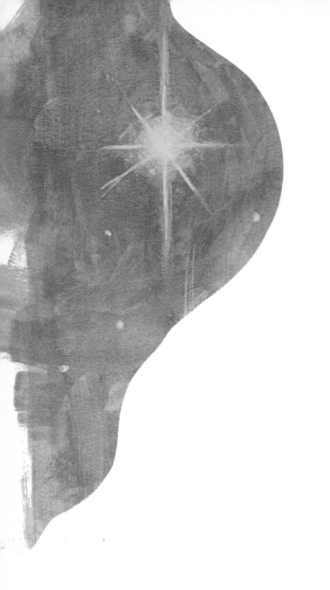

The Gift of Christmas

by Jane Belk Moncure
illustrated by Helen Endres

THE CHILD'S WORLD

ELGIN, ILLINOIS 60120

Library of Congress Cataloging in Publication Data

Moncure, Jane Belk.
   The gift of Christmas.

   (Bible story books)
   SUMMARY: Brief text retells the story of Christ's
birth in a Bethlehem stable.
      1. Jesus Christ—Nativity—Juvenile literature.
[1. Jesus Christ—Nativity. 2. Bible stories—N.T.]
I. Endres, Helen. II. Title. III. Series.
BT315.2.M63   232.9'21   79-10279
ISBN 0-89565-083-5

Distributed by Standard Publishing, 8121 Hamilton Avenue,
Cincinnati, Ohio 45231.

The Gift
of
Christmas

The Biblical account of this story
is found in *Luke 2:1-17 and
Matthew 2:1-11.*

Christmas began in Bethlehem,
a long time ago.

It began in a stable
in Bethlehem,
a long time ago.

Jesus was born
on Christmas day
and laid in a manger,
a manger of straw.

The ox and the sheep
and the little lambs saw
the Babe in the manger,
the manger of straw.

His mother, Mary,
held Him close
and praised our Heavenly Father
for the gift of Life
on Christmas day
in the manger in Bethlehem
far away.

Joseph watched over
the little Christ Child
and praised our Heavenly Father
for the gift of Love
on Christmas day
in the manger in Bethlehem
far away.

The shepherds came
and found Mary
and Joseph
and the little
Christ Child.

And they told the good news
to everyone
that a Saviour was born
in Bethlehem.

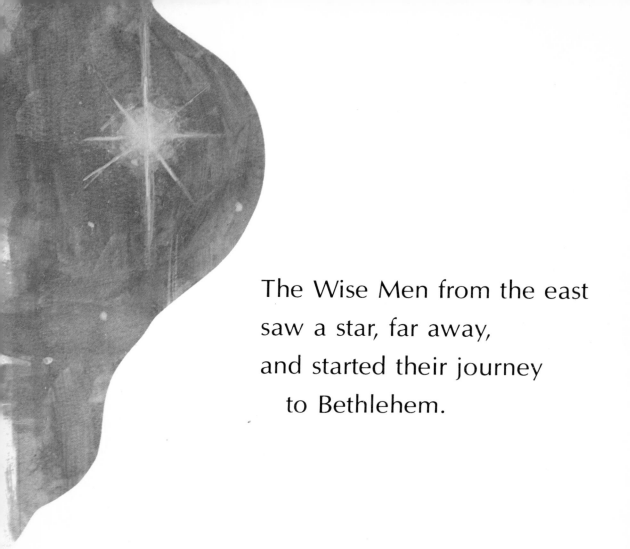

The Wise Men from the east
saw a star, far away,
and started their journey
to Bethlehem.

23

The Wise Men brought gifts
to the little Christ Child
and praised our Heavenly Father.

And all through the years
we remember the birth
of the Baby Jesus,
the first Christmas day
in a stable in Bethlehem
far away.